IT'S NOT MY FAULT, COACH !

101 EXCUSES WHY I MISSED PRACTICE

COACH MORGAN RANDALL

Coach Morgan Randall
It's Not My Fault, Coach !
Copyright © 2016 by Coach Morgan Randall

All rights reserved. No part of this book may be reproduced or transmitted in any for or by any means, electronic or mechanical, including photocopying, recording or by any information storage and retrieval system, without express written permission from the publisher, except for the inclusion of brief quotations in critical articles or a review.

The ideas expressed in this book are not in all cases, exact quotations, as some have been edited for clarity and brevity. In all cases, the author has attempted to maintain the speakers' original intent. While every effort was made to ensure accuracy of these sources, that accuracy cannot be guaranteed.

Request for permission should be made in writing or online to:

Coach Morgan Randall
Radnor University
www.CoachMorganRandall.com
info@CoachMorganRandall.com

Library of Congress Control Number: 2016917587

ISBN: 978-0-9850671-4-4
Printed in the United States of America

DEDICATION

This book is dedicated to every coach who has ever endured a horrible excuse without blowing a gasket. It's also dedicated to every coach who has been able to keep a straight face while listening to the most ludicrous or hysterical excuse ever known to man. Both make you a far better person than I.

CONTENTS

DEDICATION. iii
ACKNOWLEDGMENTS vii
INTRODUCTION. 1

    ACADEMICS 3
    LEGAL. 7
    MEDICAL 15
    ANIMALS. 27
    LOGISTICS 31
    SOCIAL 39
    GIRLFRIENDS. 45
    PSYCHOLOGICAL 51
    PERSONAL 57
    THE ABSURD 61

ABOUT THE AUTHOR. 67
ADDITIONAL RESOURCES 69
OTHER BOOKS BY COACH RANDALL. 71

ACKNOWLEDGMENTS

This book wouldn't be possible without the misguided priorities of the many student-athletes I've coached. Thanks, guys!

Oh, by the way, actually it IS your fault.

INTRODUCTION

The struggle is real, and student-athletes are no different than the rest of us. We all have days when we just don't feel like going to work, practice or anything else that remotely resembles adulting.

The list for excused absences from my practices is a very short one: death, abduction by aliens, hospitalization, an academic related school event (maybe), and that's about it. As you're about to see, the list for unexcused absences is almost infinite.

ACADEMICS

"I have Tug Barge lab."
(Yes, some people really do major in this in college.)

"I had to meet with my advisor because I'm failing gym class."

"My cinema class took a field trip to the movie theater."
($40,000 a year in tuition and they take field trips to the movie theater.)

Jon: I need to miss practice Friday and Saturday's game.

Me: Why?

Jon: I have to take a water safety exam.

Me: Remind me again which class that is for?

Jon: It's not. It's so I can be a life guard this summer.

Me: No problem. I'll trade you my whistle and a towel for all your school issued athletic equipment right now.

LEGAL

"I was mugged and all my equipment was stolen."

"The FBI was interrogating me."

"The CIA was interviewing me."
(Same kid)

(Phone call)

Kevin: Sorry I missed practice yesterday, Coach.

Me: Where the hell were you?

Kevin: I was in jail.

Me: Will you be at practice today?

Kevin: I may not be at practice for the next 5-7 years.

"I had to go to the police station and post bail for my roommate."

"I had jury duty."

"I was wrongly arrested in a case of mistaken identity."

Brian: I have a court appearance. Can I skip practice?

Me: I don't think you have a choice.

Brian: Ok. Can you skip practice and come with me?

Me: I'm the head coach, and you want me to skip my own practice? Why??

Brian: Uh, because I need a ride.

"I had an appointment with my lawyers."

** Yes, he said lawyers, as in plural.
(That means more than one.)*

"I had to drive to Maryland to
visit my dad in prison."

"I had to go take a paternity test."

Scott: I had to attend a wedding.

Me: Oh yeah, whose?

Scott: My own.

"My car was stolen, and I didn't have a ride."

(Note: He lived on a highly walkable campus which also had a free shuttle.)

"I was in a meeting with my probation officer."

"I was in a meeting with my parole officer."

(Two different kids.)

MEDICAL

"I hurt myself bowling."

"I hurt myself mini-golfing."
(Not the same kid, sadly.)

"My roommate stabbed me."
(Note: His roommate was also his teammate.)

Pete: I broke my hand reaching to grab a beer bottle that fell off the bar last night.

Me: More importantly, what happened to the beer?

Pete: Oh, don't you worry; I saved it.

Me: Well, then, that makes it an excused absence.

"My leg fell asleep while I was sitting on the toilet. When I stood up to walk I fell and broke my ankle."

"I have grass allergies, and the doctor said I can resume practice as soon as we are on AstroTurf."
(This was accompanied by a note from an allergist who coincidentally had the same last name.)

"I fell asleep in class, fell out of my desk, hit my head and got a concussion."

"My toenail fell off."

"I got carpal tunnel syndrome from an essay test I took in the morning."

"I had my wisdom teeth removed, and the dentist told me I had to relax on the couch and eat ice cream all afternoon."

Doctor's note which read:
"I'm sick and can't practice for one week."
(Yes, the handwriting matched his.)

Keith: I've been diagnosed with a severe case of "anal glaucoma".

Me: Huh? What's that mean?

Keith: It means I don't see my ass coming to practice today Coach.

"I had to go to the emergency room because I chugged a bottle of Listerine, thinking it was blue Gatorade, and got sick."

"I slept through practice, but it's not my fault. My sleeping pill looks just like my vitamin supplement."

"I can't practice because I have crabs."

(Clarification: The actual crabs were not what kept him from practicing. The fact that he treated it himself by spraying Raid on his crotch was the real culprit. He broke out in a rash which spread from his groin up to his midsection and down to his knees. That is what kept him from being able to practice. When asked why he did it, he very matter-of-factly stated "Haven't you seen the TV commercial? "Raid.... Kills bugs dead!")

"I got sunburned and am suffering from severe "heat frustration."

Billy: I have a rash "down there," and it hurts too much to run.

Me: How did you get a rash down there?

Billy: I accidentally wiped my butt with Poison Oak.

"I can't practice today because
I got my nipples pierced."

2 weeks later…

"I can't practice today because I forgot to take my nipple ring out yesterday and my nipple got ripped off."

"I practiced yesterday and can't today because I don't want to overtrain."

Ethan: I overslept yesterday.

Me: For a 7pm practice?

Ethan: I have narcolepsy.

ANIMALS

"My roommate's Akita puppy ate one of my cleats."

"I had to feed my horses."

"I can't attend morning practices because that's when I have to milk the cows."

"My dog had puppies."

"I had to turn a paper in but my dog ate my thumb drive. So I had to follow him around the yard for a couple hours, if you know what I mean."

"I got sprayed by a skunk."

"My dog ate my cup,
so I can't practice today."

"Sorry I missed practice; the fish were biting real good yesterday, and I didn't want to leave the lake. Did you get my voicemail I left inviting you to join us?"

LOGISTICS

"The weather was bad."
(Note: It was lightly raining and practice was indoors)

Me: Where were you yesterday, Tim?

Tim: You said we have practice in two days not yesterday.

Me: I said we have two-a-days!

"I can't train properly.
The gym is too crowded."

"I can't train properly.
The gym is too empty."

(Same kid)

"It's Sunday, and the Lord said this is supposed to be a day of rest."

"It's Monday. Come on Coach, you know nobody gets anything done on Mondays."

"It's Tuesday."

"It's Wednesday."

"It's Thursday."

"It's Friday."

"It's Saturday."

"The traffic was horrible; hopefully,
tomorrow will be better,
but I wouldn't count on it."

"You didn't get my voicemail that
I was just going to practice
at home yesterday?"

"It was too cold."

"It was too hot."

(Same kid)

"I couldn't unlock my locker."

SOCIAL

"I was Christmas shopping."
(In October?)

"My house was hosting a toga party we had to get ready for."

"The new Harry Potter book just came out today, so I waited in line to get one of the limited edition copies."

Brad: I can't come to practice tomorrow; I have tickets to see Pearl Jam.

Me: I don't care.

Brad: You don't understand Coach, I'd skip my grandmother's funeral to see Pearl Jam.

Me: You told me you had to miss practice last month because your grandmother died.

(She also died twice before that, apparently.)

Mike: I have tickets to a Flyers game.

Me: I don't care.

Mike: But, coach, they're glass seats.

Me: I don't care if the seats are Waterford Crystal.

Mike: Huh?

Todd: Our frat is having a beach themed barbecue tonight and I'm the party chairman. Tons of hot chicks in bikinis and free beer. Want to join us, Coach?

Me: Todd, please tell everyone practice is cancelled. It sounds like you need me to chaperone.

GIRLFRIENDS

Darin: My girlfriend is pregnant.

Me: Is she in labor?

Darin: No, that's not for another nine months, Coach.

"My girlfriend's boyfriend came home unexpectedly, and I was stuck hiding under their bed."

"I had to go to a prom out of state."
(His girlfriend was a junior in high school. He was a senior… in college.)

"I can't practice; I threw my back out this weekend. It's probably from my girlfriend and me doing it on the floor."

Rich: I can't come to practice because I'm upset.

Me: Why are your upset?

Rich: Because my girlfriend broke up with me.

Me: That's your reason? Now I'm upset. How about we let you cry during water breaks, then will you come to practice?

Brian: I can't come to practice because I have to pick up my girlfriend up the airport.

Me: You have a girlfriend?

Brian: Sort of. She's 35, lives in another country and is married to a Federal Agent.

(Which means there's about a 0.001% chance they didn't meet online.)

"I couldn't come to practice because I found out my girlfriend was cheating on me, so my roommates and I performed a sting operation."

"My girlfriend caught me cheating on her, threw all my stuff away and I had to dig all my belongings out of the garbage."

PSYCHOLOGICAL

"I forgot what day it was."

"I couldn't find the practice field."

"My girlfriend's sorority house is haunted, and one of the ghosts kept me up all night."

"I was in the equipment room getting a new helmet. The face mask on my old one was making me claustrophobic."

"I had back-to-back appointments with my psychologist and then my psychiatrist."

"My appointment with my shrink took longer than I expected."

"I was suddenly struck with a case of agoraphobia and couldn't leave the house."

"I woke up, didn't know where I was, and thought it was Sunday."

Tony: I forgot to change my clock to spring ahead to day light savings time.

Me: So, shouldn't you have been an hour early for practice, instead of missing it completely?

(Tony was a math major.)

PERSONAL

"I was hung over."

"I was too drunk to practice."

"I can't come to practice because my barber shop quartet practice is at the same time."

"Practice conflicted with happy hour and I'm Irish."

Jason: I was on the toilet.

Me: The whole two hours?

Jason: Coach, you've eaten at the cafeteria before, right?

"It was after my bedtime."

"It was my birthday."

"I had a very important party to go to…
my cousin's bar mitzvah"

THE ABSURD

"I'm thinking of transferring and was visiting with another college coach at his school."

"I have to attend our tribe's annual Sweat Lodge ceremony all weekend."

(In all my years, this is my personal favorite.)

"I have tickets to see Neil Diamond."

(Note: This was in 1999, not 1979)

"I didn't have a ride to practice."

(Said player lived on campus NEXT TO THE PRACTICE FIELD.)

"The team physician told me I needed more vitamin D, so I skipped practice to go to the beach."

"I was busy getting my hair cut."

"I couldn't get the car out of the garage, because the power was out, so the garage door wouldn't open."

"Sorry I missed practice.
I was trying out for another team."

"I put my practice uniform in the
microwave to dry, and it caught fire."

"I worked so hard in the game Saturday; I thought I earned the day off practice yesterday."

"I woke up from my afternoon nap in a good mood, and I didn't want to ruin it."

ABOUT THE AUTHOR

Morgan Randall is a great American philosopher, coach, mentor and legend (in his own mind). He has been leading teams at Radnor University for over forty years and has no plans on retiring any time soon. In 2012 the Radnor University administration awarded him a lifetime contract. It's the only award he has ever wanted.

While he has hundreds of wins to his credit, Coach Randall is a member of zero halls of fame and has no interest in belonging to any organization that would have him as a member. According to Randall *"coaching is about the rewards not the awards and the rewards are in the relationships".*

More information is available at: **CoachMorganRandall.com**

ADDITIONAL RESOURCES

- Do you have an uncontrollable urge to sleep through practice?
- Do you frequently struggle to find the motivation to attend practice?

If so, you may be suffering from a condition known as EPA or Excessive Practice Absence. These symptoms also coincide with: difficulty holding yourself accountable, not understanding your role and shirking responsibility on your team. For help treating your case of EPA go to:

AccountabilityIssues.com

OTHER BOOKS BY COACH RANDALL

If you've enjoyed reading *It's Not My Fault, Coach!* you will also love the many other books in the Participation Trophy Book series by Coach Morgan Randall. More information is available at: **ParticipationTrophyBooks.com**

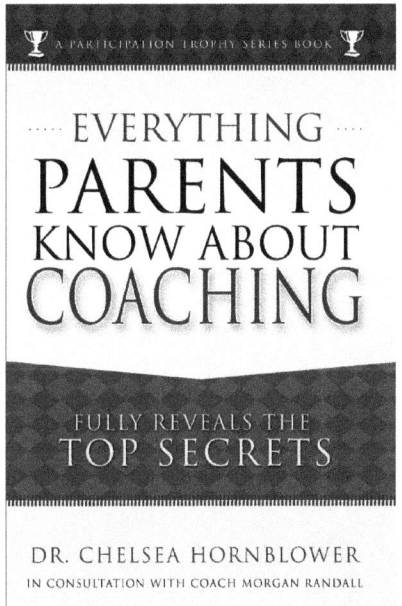

www.ingramcontent.com/pod-product-compliance
Lightning Source LLC
Chambersburg PA
CBHW050705160426
43194CB00010B/2006